Baby A

by Wiley Blevins

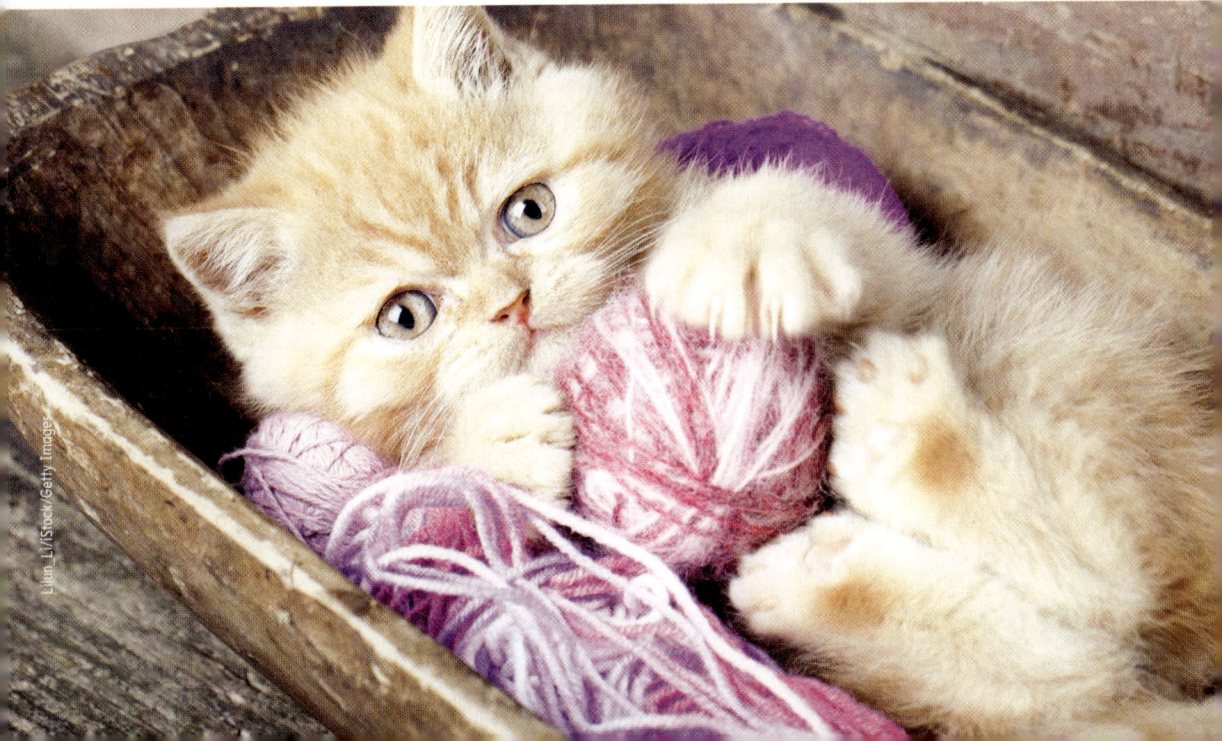

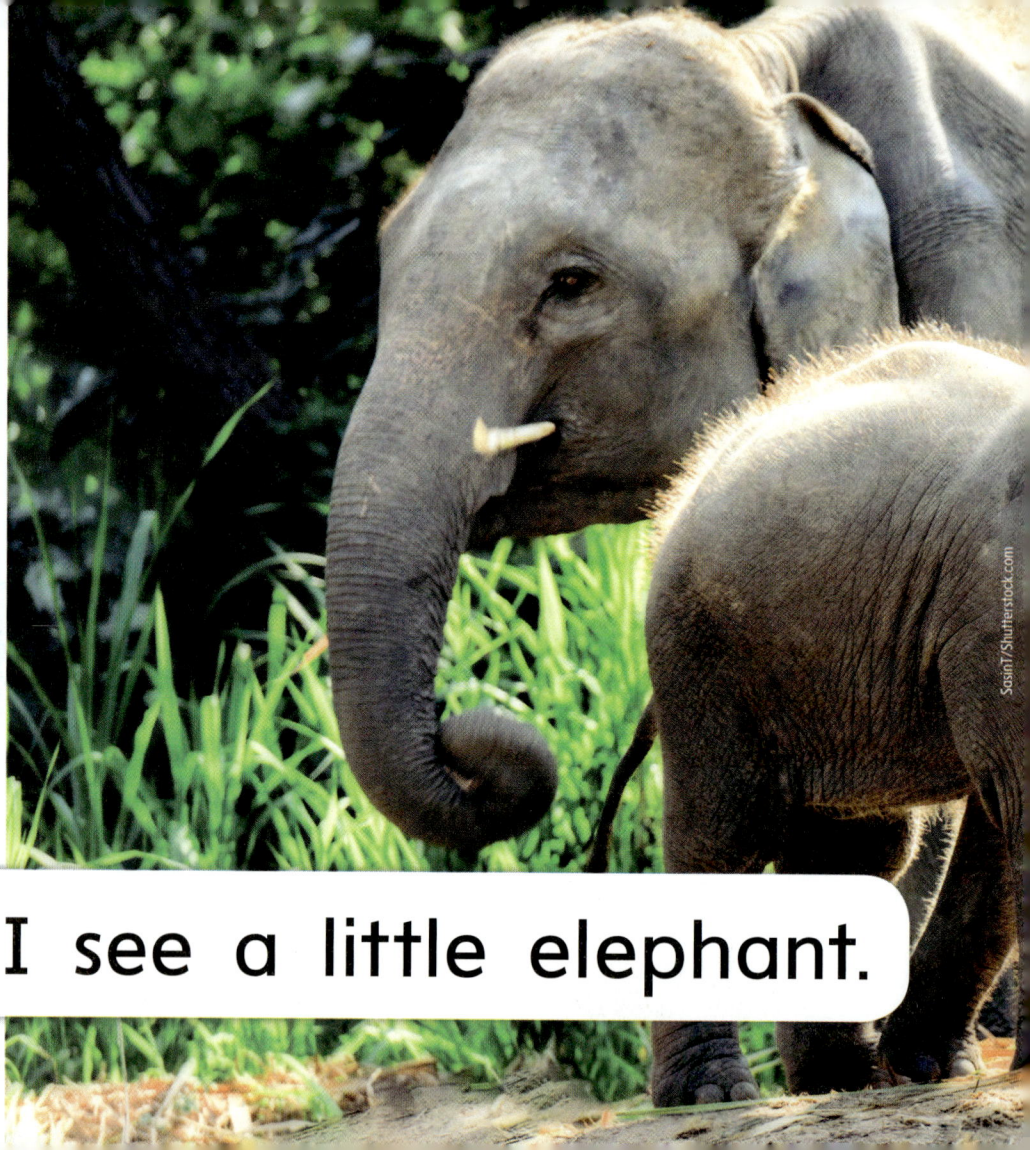

I see a little elephant.

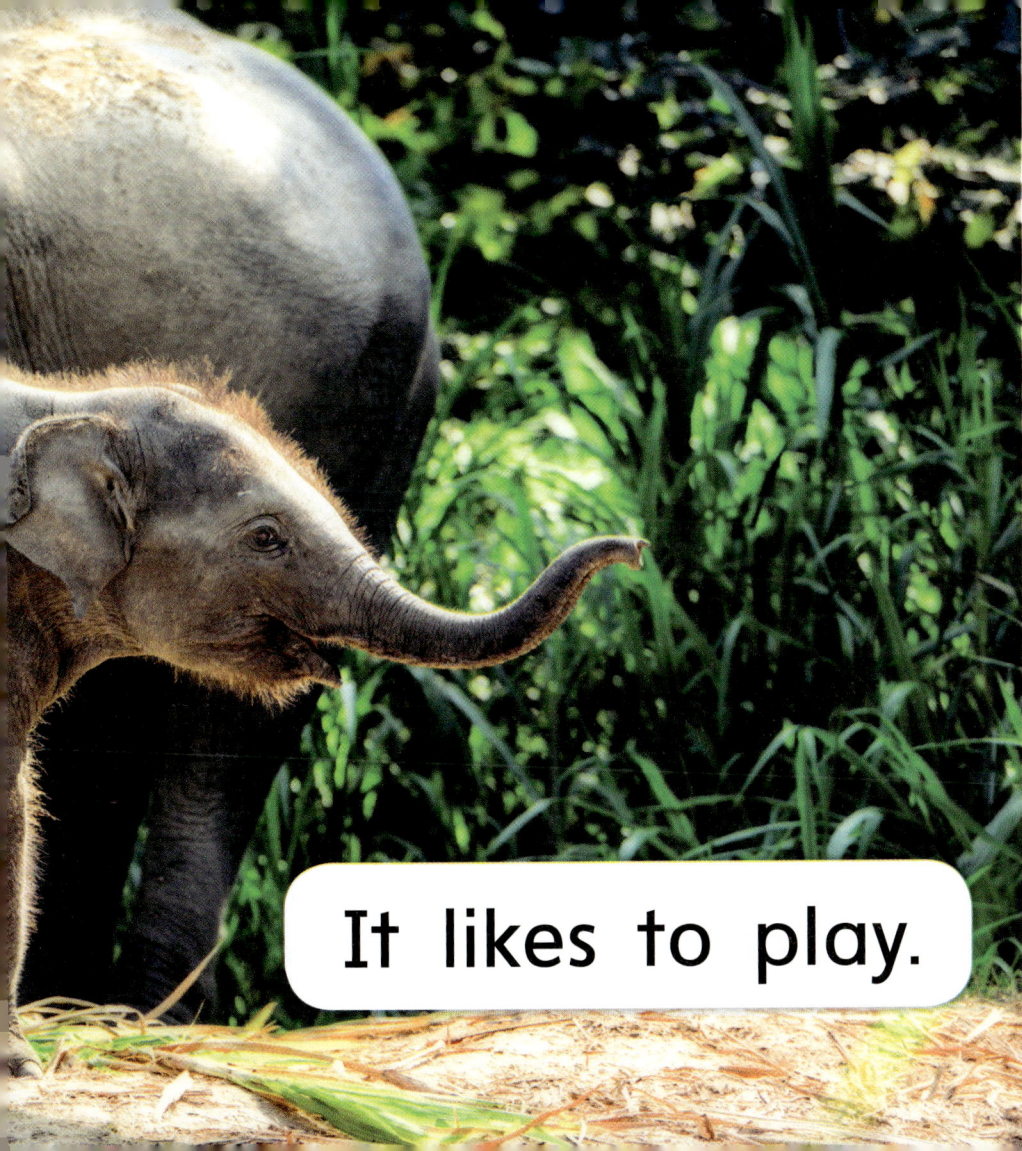

It likes to play.

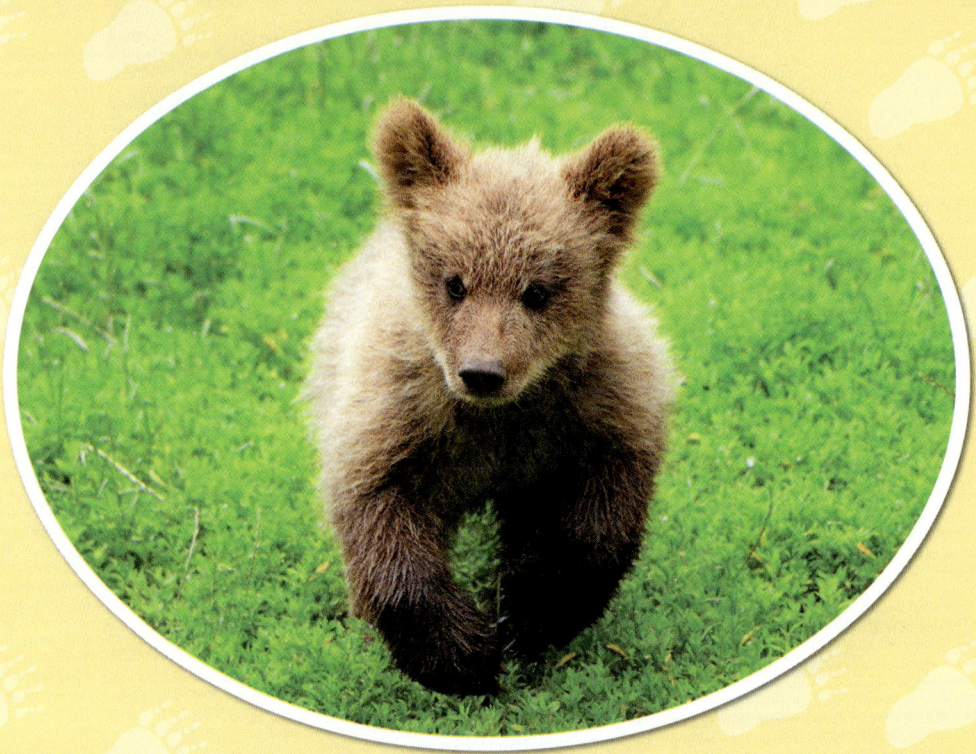

I see a little bear.

©Raimund Linke/Getty Images

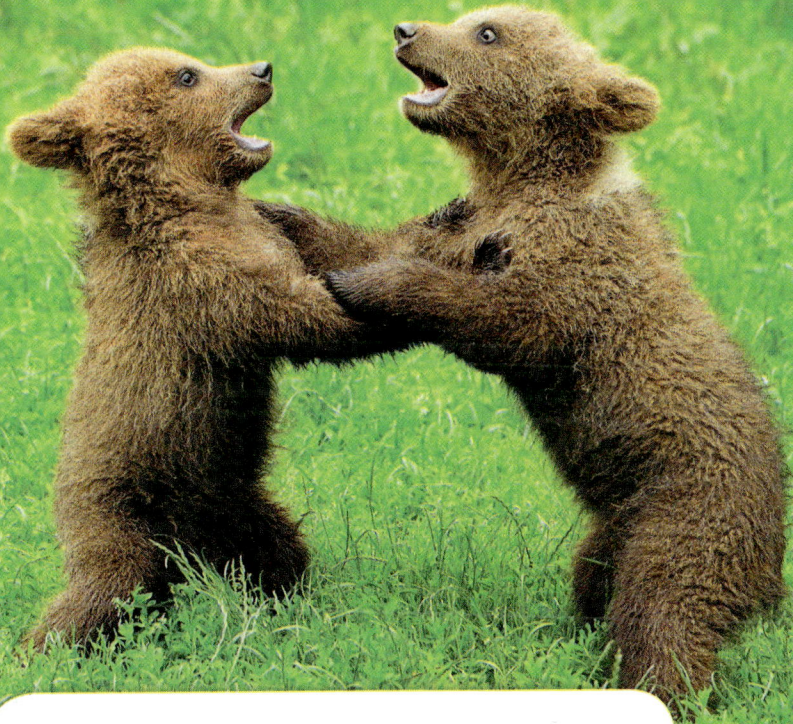

It likes to play.

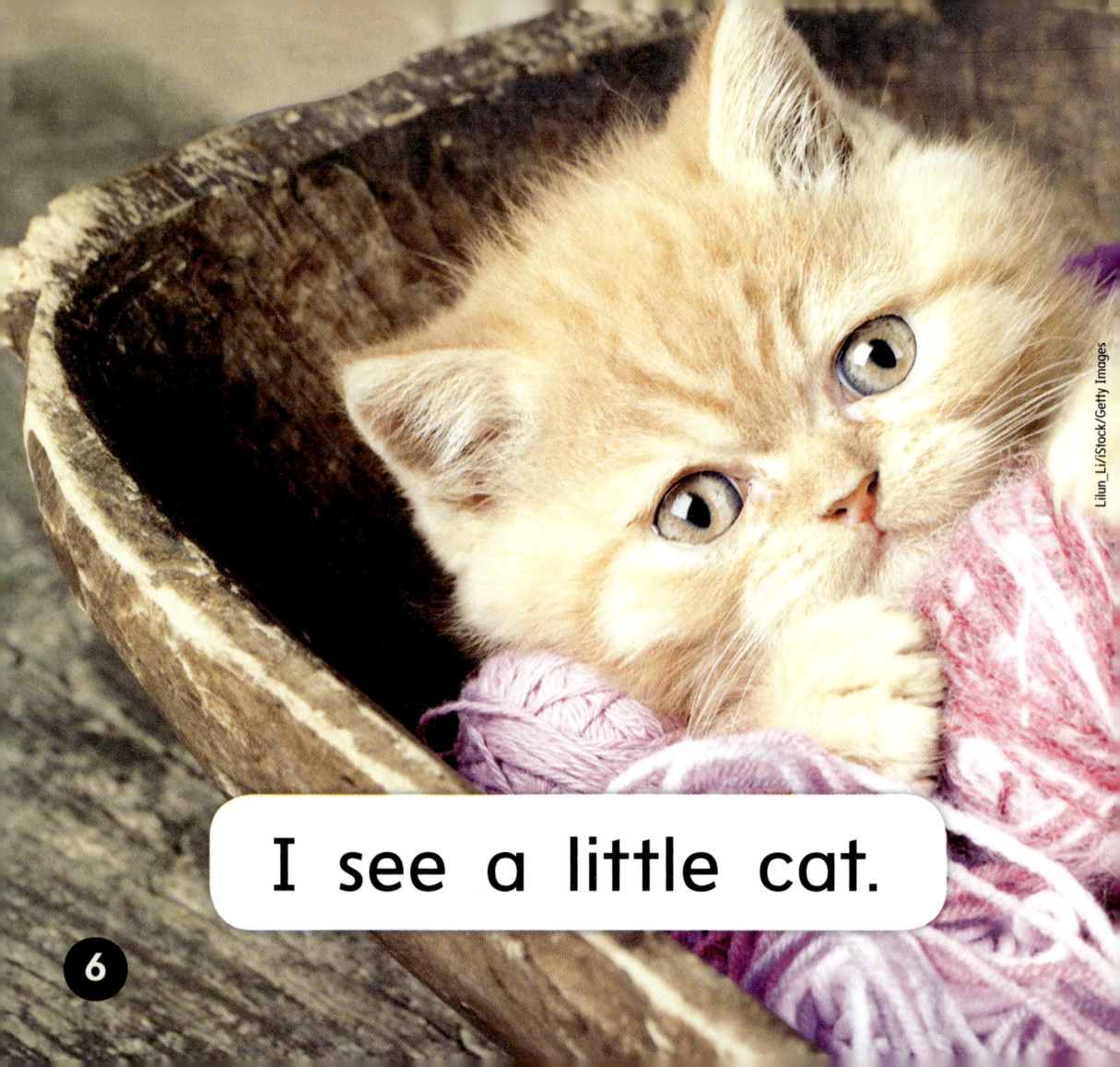

I see a little cat.

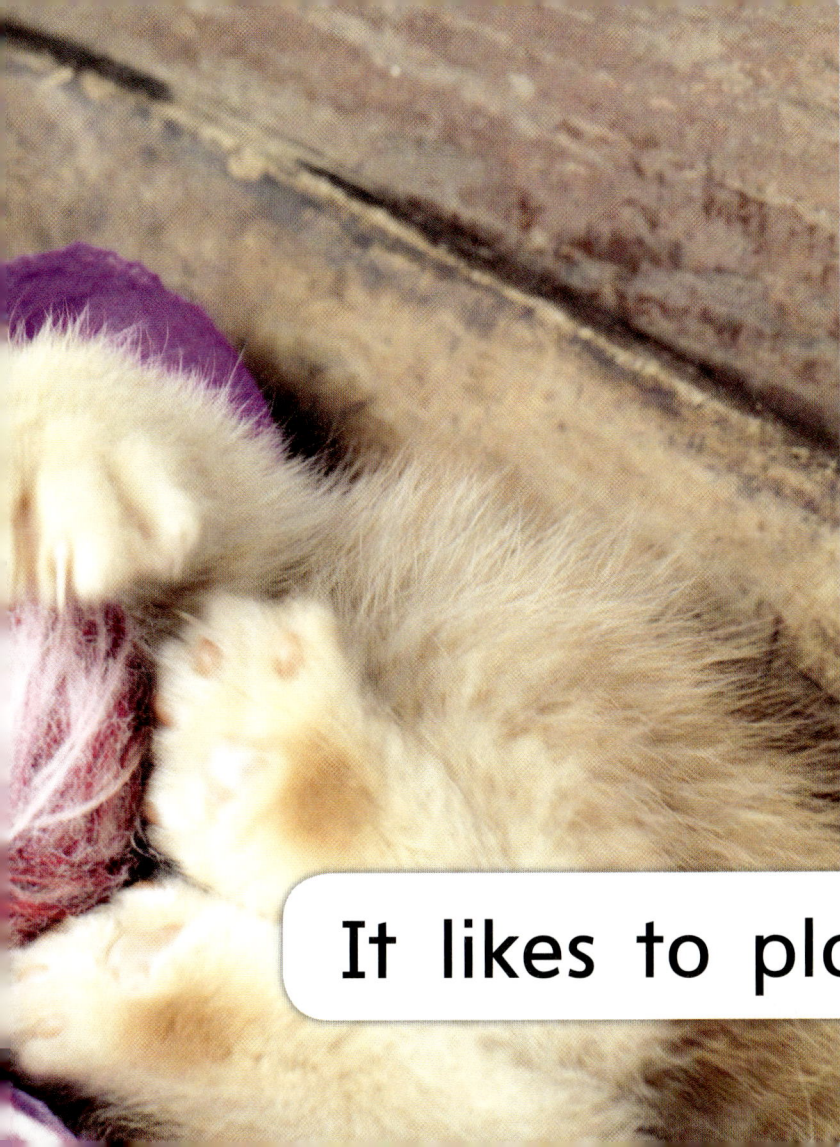

It likes to play.

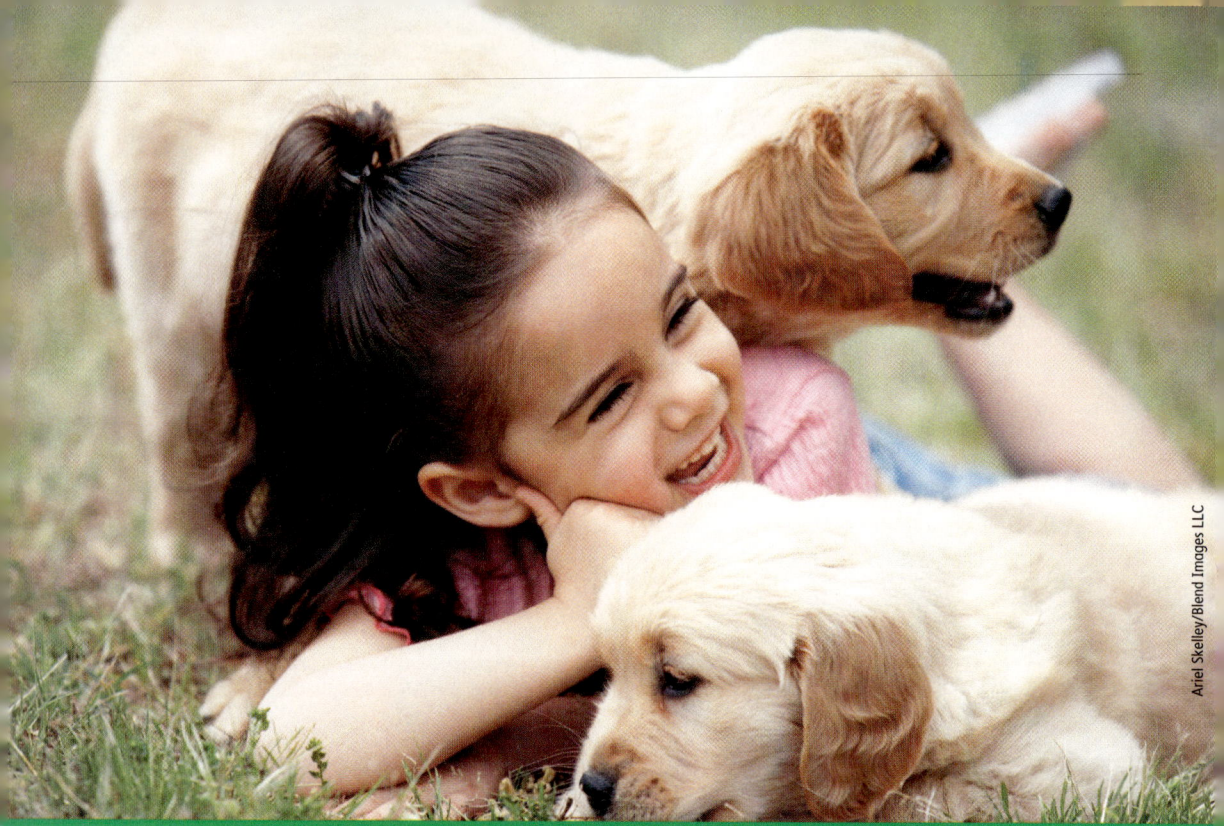

I see a little dog.
It likes me!

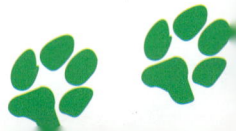

8